Rooted in Faith

31 Bible Verses and Positive Affirmations to Start Your Morning

Tasha (TC) Cooper

UpwardAction Media
Washington DC

Rooted in Faith
31 Bible Verses and Positive Affirmations to Start Your Morning

About FaithFocusFlow® International

FaithFocusFlow® International is a movement for founders, owners, and leaders committed to building businesses and corporate cultures that serve people, create wealthy legacies, and glorify Christ.

We provide bible reading plans, books, events, and digital programs to help you strengthen your Christ-centered, biblically-sound business thinking to help you make decisions in all circumstances that reflect the character of Christ. FaithFocusFlow® International has the strategies, formulas, and tools that you need to make marketplaces and workspaces here on earth more like heaven.

Learn more about FaithFocusFlow® International and how you can get involved on our website at www. FaithFocusFlow.com.

About FaithFocusFlow®
Institute for Leaders

The FaithFocusFlow® Institute for Leader's website is a digital campus designed with you in mind.

We've curated a virtual experience that makes it easy to find programs, download resources, and connect with like-minded leaders.

Here's more of what's available to our clients:

- Business-Focused Bible Reading Plans
- Masterclasses
- Business Accelerators
- Virtual Co-Working Experiences
- Group Coaching Opportunities

Learn more about FaithFocusFlow® International and how you can get involved on our website at www.FaithFocusFlow.com.

Let's stay connected!

Let's stay connected!

Share your challenges and victories with us as you use this journal on your journey to becoming your very best self. We want to be virtually with you celebrating your wins, and praying with you through the challenges.

Use the hashtag **#RootInFaithJournal** to tag us in your posts on Instagram, Facebook, and Twitter.

The information you share on social media may be just the inspiration the person reading your post needs to help get deeper rooted in their faith.

⃝	https://www.instagram.com/FaithFocusFlow
f	https://www.facebook.com/FaithFocusFlow
ⓟ	https://www.pinterest.com/FaithFocusFlow
t	https://twitter.com/FaithFocusFlow
🌐	https://www.FaithFocusFlow.com/YouTube

Subscribe to Our Daily eLetter

Get Christ-centered, bible-based, business lessons delivered to your inbox on weekday mornings!

Be inspired, encouraged, and empowered to do the Work God created you to do by reading our weekday publication - *The FAITHgineer™ eLetter.*

Subscribe at absolutely no cost to you at www.FaithFocusFlow.com/eLetter.

It's our gift to you!

Welcome!

Welcome to the *Rooted in Faith: 31 Bible Verses and Positive Affirmations to Start Your Morning* Journal.

I created this journal to be a resource for your daily morning prayer and meditation practice. Use it to inspire your morning routine of prayer and meditation.

This journal is designed to make it easy for you to write down your thoughts, feelings, and revelations during your morning routine. I hope the bible verses and affirmations contained herein will help you become more firmly rooted in your faith than ever before.

Let these verses and affirmations help center your thoughts on biblically, Christ-centered truths, and stay connected to the grace and mercy of our Lord and Savior Jesus Christ. When you are connected to Christ, you can dial into the power you have through the presence of Holy Spirit - who dwells inside of you.

I intend for every single Bible verse and affirmation contained in this journal to help you increase your courage, strengthen your confidence, and tap into the power of Holy Spirit. Here's why - So that you can more powerfully, effectively, efficiently, and profitably do the good works created for YOU before you were even born.

Use this daily journal and guide to transform your business and your life.

Rooted in Faith and Rooting for You!

TC Cooper

TC Cooper, Founder
FaithFocusFlow® Institute for Leaders

Getting Started

As I prepare myself for the next 31 days, I pray and expect

....

....

....

....

....

....

....

....

....

....

....

....

Bible Verse 1

Be alert and of sober mind. Your enemy, the devil,
prowls around like a roaring lion looking for
someone to devour.

1 Peter 5:8 (NIV)

Today's Affirmation

I am alert and attentive. I am ready to slay everything that
comes my way.

This morning, I

....

....

....

....

....

....

....

....

....

....

....

....

....

....

....

Bible Verse 2

Let the morning bring me word of your unfailing love,
for I have put my trust in you. Show me the way
I should go, for to you I entrust my life.

Psalm 143:8 (NIV)

Today's Affirmation

God guides my path. I trust Him with my life.

This morning, I

....

....

....

....

....

....

....

....

....

....

....

....

....

....

....

Bible Verse 3

Because of the Lord's great love we are not consumed,
for his compassions never fail. They are new every
morning; great is your faithfulness.

Lamentations 3:22-23 (NIV)

Today's Affirmation

I am consumed by the love, faithfulness, and compassion
of Jesus Christ.

This morning, I

....

....

....

....

....

....

....

....

....

....

....

....

....

....

....

Bible Verse 4

In the morning, Lord, you hear my voice;
in the morning I lay my request before
you and wait expectantly.

Psalm 5:3 (NIV)

Today's Affirmation

The Lord hears my cries, and all things are working for my good.

This morning, I

....

....

....

....

....

....

....

....

....

....

....

....

....

....

....

Bible Verse 5

I will instruct you and teach you in the way
you should go; I will counsel you with
my eye upon you.

Psalm 32:8 (ESV)

Today's Affirmation

God sees me, knows my needs, and counsels me through
wisdom in scripture.

This morning, I

....

....

....

....

....

....

....

....

....

....

....

....

....

....

....

Bible Verse 6

For his anger lasts only a moment, but his favor,
a lifetime. Weeping may stay overnight,
but there is joy in the morning.

Psalm 30:5 (CSB)

Today's Affirmation

I am covered with favor and joy from the Lord.

This morning, I

....

....

....

....

....

....

....

....

....

....

....

....

....

....

....

Bible Verse 7

But remember that the Lord your God gives you the power to gain wealth, in order to confirm his covenant he swore to your fathers, as it is today.

Deuteronomy 8:18 (CSB)

Today's Affirmation

God gives me the ability to create wealth.

This morning, I

....

....

....

....

....

....

....

....

....

....

....

....

....

....

....

Bible Verse 8

Teach us to number our days carefully so that we may develop wisdom in our hearts.

Psalm 90:12 (CSB)

Today's Affirmation

I will be intentional about today and wise with my time.

This morning, I

....

....

....

....

....

....

....

....

....

....

....

....

....

....

....

Bible Verse 9

Satisfy us in the morning with your faithful love so
that we may shout with joy and be glad all our days.

Psalm 90:14 (CSB)

Today's Affirmations

Christ deeply loves me; His steadfast love for me renews
every morning.

This morning, I

....

....

....

....

....

....

....

....

....

....

....

....

....

....

Bible Verse 10

I will say concerning the Lord, who is my refuge
and my fortress, my God in whom I trust:
He himself will rescue you from the bird trap,
from the destructive plague.

Psalm 91:2 (CSB)

Today's Affirmation

I trust God. He is my refuge and my fortress.

This morning, I

....

....

....

....

....

....

....

....

....

....

....

....

....

....

....

Bible Verse 11

The Lord God has given me the tongue of those who
are instructed to know how to sustain the
weary with a word. He awakens me each morning;
he awakens my ear to listen like those
being instructed.

Isaiah 50:4 (CSB)

Accompanying Affirmation

I listen to God, and I carry with me a Word to encourage
the weary.

This morning, I

....

....

....

....

....

....

....

....

....

....

....

....

....

....

....

Bible Verse 12

Do not forsake wisdom, and she will protect you;
love her, and she will watch over you.

Proverbs 4:6 (NIV)

Today's Affirmation

Wisdom watches over me and protects me from lasting harm.

This morning, I

....

....

....

....

....

....

....

....

....

....

....

....

....

....

....

Bible Verse 13

For you were called to be free, brother and sisters; only
don't use this freedom as an opportunity for the flesh,
but serve one another through love.

Galatians 5:13 (CSB)

Today's Affirmation

I am called to be free! I serve those who encounter my
Work or me through my love in action.

This morning, I

....

....

....

....

....

....

....

....

....

....

....

....

....

....

....

Bible Verse 14

I will go before you and will level the uneven places;
I will shatter the bronze doors and cut
the iron bars in two.

Isaiah 45:2

Today's Affirmation

God goes before me; I follow His lead.

This morning, I

....

....

....

....

....

....

....

....

....

....

....

....

....

....

....

Bible Verse 15

"Follow me," Jesus told them,
"and I will make you fish for people."

Mark 1:17 (CSB)

Today's Affirmation

My actions at Work *in my job, business, or career* inspire
people to learn more about Jesus.

This morning, I

....

....

....

....

....

....

....

....

....

....

....

....

....

....

....

Bible Verse 16

They were astonished at his teaching because
he was teaching them as one who had authority
and not like the scribes.

Mark 1:22 (CSB)

Today's Affirmation

I lead with courage and confidence *(not arrogance)* under
the authority of Jesus.

This morning, I

....

....

....

....

....

....

....

....

....

....

....

....

....

....

....

Bible Verse 17

Very early in the morning, while it was still dark,
he got up, went out, and made his way to a deserted
place; and there he was praying.

Mark 1:35 (CSB)

Today's Affirmation

I arise early in the morning to pray and meditate before
the Lord.

This morning, I

....

....

....

....

....

....

....

....

....

....

....

....

....

....

....

Bible Verse 18

The mouths of the righteous utter wisdom and their
tongues speak what is just.

Psalm 37:30 (NIV)

Today's Affirmation

I speak life. My words are wise and just.

This morning, I

....

....

....

....

....

....

....

....

....

....

....

....

....

....

....

Bible Verse 19

I rise before dawn and cry for help;
I have put my hope in your word.

Psalm 119:147 (NIV)

Today's Affirmation

I am at peace. My hope rests in the Lord.

This morning, I

....

....

....

....

....

....

....

....

....

....

....

....

....

....

....

Bible Verse 20

But seek first the kingdom of God and his
righteousness, and all these things
will be provided for you.

Matthew 6:33 (CSB)

Today's Affirmation

I intentionally seek the righteousness of God in my every
decision and interaction.

This morning, I

....

....

....

....

....

....

....

....

....

....

....

....

....

....

....

Bible Verse 21

For God loved the world in this way. He gave his one and
only Son, so that everyone who believes in him will not
perish but have eternal life.

John 3:16 (CSB)

Today's Affirmation

I cannot lose. Christ has given me eternal life.

This morning, I

....

....

....

....

....

....

....

....

....

....

....

....

....

....

....

Bible Verse 22

Lord, be gracious to us! We wait for you.
Be our strength every morning and our salvation
in times of trouble.

Isaiah 33:2 (CSB)

Today's Affirmation

The Lord is my strength every day, throughout my day.

This morning, I

....

....

....

....

....

....

....

....

....

....

....

....

....

....

....

Bible Verse 23

Commit to the Lord whatever you do,
and he will establish your plans.

Proverbs 16:3 (NIV)

Today's Affirmation

I am committed to Work that serves people and glorifies
God. I consult with God when planning my work, and He
establishes my plans.

This morning, I

....

....

....

....

....

....

....

....

....

....

....

....

....

....

....

Bible Verse 24

Your word is a lamp for my feet, a light on my path.

Psalm 119:105 (NIV)

Accompanying Affirmation

I study scripture and apply its guidance throughout my day.

This morning, I

....

....

....

....

....

....

....

....

....

....

....

....

....

....

....

Bible Verse 25

This is the day the Lord has made; let us rejoice
and be glad in it.

Psalm 118:24 (NIV)

Today's Affirmation

Today is my day. I'm winning it all.

This morning, I

....

....

....

....

....

....

....

....

....

....

....

....

....

....

....

Bible Verse 26

Trust in the Lord with all your heart,
and do not rely on your own understanding.

Proverbs 3:5 (CSB)

Today's Affirmation

I trust the Lord when things do not seem fair.

I trust the Lord when I do not understand.

I trust the Lord at all times.

This morning, I

....

....

....

....

....

....

....

....

....

....

....

....

....

....

....

Bible Verse 27

Plans fail when there is no counsel,
but with many advisers they succeed.

Proverbs 15:22 (CSB)

Today's Affirmation

I am attracting Christ-centered advisers to advise me in doing my Work and living my best life.

This morning, I

....

....

....

....

....

....

....

....

....

....

....

....

....

....

....

Bible Verse 28

Just as each one has received a gift,
use it to serve others, as good stewards
of the varied grace of God.

1 Peter 4:10 (CSB)

Today's Affirmation

I am using my gifts to serve people in the world around
me and beyond.

This morning, I

....

....

....

....

....

....

....

....

....

....

....

....

....

....

....

Bible Verse 29

Teach me your way, Lord, and I will live by your truth.
Give me an undivided mind to fear your name.

Psalm 86:11 (CSB)

Today's Affirmation

My courage and confidence is built on the truth of what
God says about me and what I can do through the power
that lives inside of me.

This morning, I

....

....

....

....

....

....

....

....

....

....

....

....

....

....

....

Bible Verse 30

Listen to the sound of my pleading when I cry to
you for help, when I lift up my hands toward
your holy sanctuary.

Psalm 28:2

Today's Affirmation

I lift my hands in total praise as I cry out for help, and I do
it filled with confidence that God will respond.

This morning, I

....

....

....

....

....

....

....

....

....

....

....

....

....

....

....

Bible Verse 31

Wisdom is supreme - so get wisdom.
And whatever else you get, get understanding.

Proverbs 4:7 (CSB)

Today's Affirmation

I am intentional, and my life is blessed with wisdom and
understanding.

This morning, I

....

....

....

....

....

....

....

....

....

....

....

....

....

....

You did it!

Congratulations on investing 31 days in prayer, meditation, and reflection.

Let's do a quick assessment.

- What's different in your life and Work?
- How did God show up for you?
- How did you show up for your self?
- What will you change during the next 31 days?

....

....

....

....

....

....

....

....

....

....

....

....

....

....

....

....

....

....

....

We want to hear from you!

Tell us about your transformation. Share on social media and use the hashtag **#ALIGNplanner** or email us at WeCare@FaithFocusFlow.

We can not wait to read your stories!

Appendix 1: Bible Verses

We've included all of the bible verses listed in this journal to help you reflect upon what you learned about God and yourself during the preceding 31 days.

Do the journal work first, then use this list to review.

Day 1	Be alert and of sober mind. Your enemy, the devil, prowls around like a roaring lion looking for someone to devour.	1 Peter 5:8 (NIV)
Day 2	Let the morning bring me word of your unfailing love, for I have put my trust in you. Show me the way I should go, for to you I entrust my life.	Psalm 143:8 (NIV)
Day 3	Because of the Lord's great love we are not consumed, for his compassions never fail. They are new every morning; great is your faithfulness.	Lamentations 3:22-23 (NIV)
Day 4	In the morning, Lord, you hear my voice; in the morning I lay my request before you and wait expectantly.	Psalm 5:3 (NIV)

Day 5	I will instruct you and teach you in the way you should go; I will counsel you with my eye upon you.	Psalm 32:8 (ESV)
Day 6	For his anger lasts only a moment, but his favor, a lifetime. Weeping may stay overnight, but there is joy in the morning.	Psalm 30:5 (CSB)
Day 7	But remember that the Lord your God gives you the power to gain wealth, in order to confirm his covenant he swore to your fathers, as it is today.	Deuteronomy 8:18 (CSB)
Day 8	Teach us to number our days carefully so that we may develop wisdom in our hearts.	Psalm 90:12 (CSB)
Day 9	Satisfy us in the morning with your faithful love so that we may shout with joy and be glad all our days.	Psalm 90:14 (CSB)
Day 10	I will say concerning the Lord, who is my refuge and my fortress, my God in whom I trust: He himself will rescue you from the bird trap, from the destructive plague.	Psalm 91:2 (CSB)

Day 11	The Lord God has given me the tongue of those who are instructed to know how to sustain the weary with a word. He awakens me each morning; he awakens my ear to listen like those being instructed.	Isaiah 50:4 (CSB)
Day 12	Do not forsake wisdom, and she will protect you; love her, and she will watch over you.	Proverbs 4:6 (NIV)
Day 13	For you were called to be free, brother and sisters; only don't use this freedom as an opportunity for the flesh, but serve one another through love.	Galatians 5:13 (CSB)
Day 14	I will go before you and will level the uneven places; I will shatter the bronze doors and cut the iron bars in two.	Isaiah 45:2 (NIV)
Day 15	"Follow me," Jesus told them, "and I will make you fish for people."	Mark 1:17 (CSB)
Day 16	They were astonished at his teaching because he was teaching them as one who had authority and not like the scribes.	Mark 1:22 (CSB)

Day 17	Very early in the morning, while it was still dark, he got up, went out, and made his way to a deserted place; and there he was praying.	Mark 1:35 (CSB)
Day 18	The mouths of the righteous utter wisdom and their tongues speak what is just.	Psalm 37:30 (NIV)
Day 19	I rise before dawn and cry for help; I have put my hope in your word.	Psalm 119:147 (NIV)
Day 20	But seek first the kingdom of God and his righteousness, and all these things will be provided for you.	Matthew 6:33 (CSB)
Day 21	For God loved the world in this way. He gave his one and only Son, so that everyone who believes in him will not perish but have eternal life.	John 3:16 (CSB)
Day 22	Lord, be gracious to us! We wait for you. Be our strength every morning and our salvation in times of trouble.	Isaiah 33:2 (CSB)
Day 23	Commit to the Lord whatever you do, and he will establish your plans.	Proverbs 16:3 (NIV)
Day 24	Your word is a lamp for my feet, a light on my path.	Psalm 119:105 (NIV)

Day 25	This is the day the Lord has made; let us rejoice and be glad in it.	Psalm 118:24 (NIV)
Day 26	Trust in the Lord with all your heart, and do not rely on your own understanding.	Proverbs 3:5 (CSB)
Day 27	Plans fail when there is no counsel, but with many advisers they succeed.	Proverbs 15:22 (CSB)
Day 28	Just as each one has received a gift, use it to serve others, as good stewards of the varied grace of God.	1 Peter 4:10 (CSB)
Day 29	Teach me your way, Lord, and I will live by your truth. Give me an undivided mind to fear your name.	Psalm 86:11 (CSB)
Day 30	Listen to the sound of my pleading when I cry to you for help, when I lift up my hands toward your holy sanctuary.	Psalm 28:2 (CSB)
Day 31	Wisdom is supreme - so get wisdom. And whatever else you get, get understanding.	Proverbs 4:7 (CSB)

Appendix 2: Daily Affirmations

After you have invested 31 days journaling your revelations, insight, and new awareness through meditation and affirmation, use this appendix to continue your personal growth as you increase your faith, focus, and flow.

Day 1	I am alert and attentive. I am ready to slay everything that comes my way.
Day 2	God guides my path. I trust Him with my life.
Day 3	I am consumed by the love, faithfulness, and compassion of Jesus Christ.
Day 4	The Lord hears my cries, and all things are working for my good.
Day 5	God sees me, knows my needs, and counsels me through wisdom in scripture.
Day 6	I am covered with favor and joy from the Lord.
Day 7	God gives me the ability to create wealth.
Day 8	I will be intentional about today and wise with my time.
Day 9	Christ deeply loves me; His steadfast love for me renews every morning.
Day 10	I trust God. He is my refuge and my fortress.

Day 11	I listen to God, and I carry with me a Word to encourage the weary.
Day 12	Wisdom watches over me and protects me from lasting harm.
Day 13	I am called to be free! I serve those who encounter my Work or me through my love in action.
Day 14	God goes before me; I follow His lead.
Day 15	My actions at Work in my job, business, or career inspire people to learn more about Jesus.
Day 16	I lead with courage and confidence (not arrogance) under the authority of Jesus.
Day 17	I arise early in the morning to pray and meditate before the Lord.
Day 18	I speak life. My words are wise and just.
Day 19	I am at peace. My hope rests in the Lord.
Day 20	I intentionally seek the righteousness of God in my every decision and interaction.
Day 21	I cannot lose. Christ has given me eternal life.
Day 22	The Lord is my strength every day, throughout my day.
Day 23	I am committed to Work that serves people and glorifies God. I consult with God when planning my work, and He establishes my plans.

Day 24	I study scripture and apply its guidance throughout my day.
Day 25	Today is my day. I'm winning it all.
Day 26	I trust the Lord when things do not seem fair. I trust the Lord when I do not understand. I trust the Lord at all times.
Day 27	I am attracting Christ-centered advisers to advise me in doing my Work and living my best life.
Day 28	I am using my gifts to serve people in the world around me and beyond.
Day 29	My courage and confidence is built on the truth of what God says about me and what I can do through the power that lives inside of me.
Day 30	I lift my hands in total praise as I cry out for help, and I do it filled with confidence that God will respond.
Day 31	I am intentional, and my life is blessed with wisdom and understanding.

FAITHFOCUSFLOW®
INSTITUTE FOR LEADERS

Our award-winning programs are designed, developed, and built to help founders, owners, leaders, and change-makers (aka Faithgineers™) be excellent in three key areas:

Christ-Centered Decision-Making:
Align all decisions with biblical principles using our proprietary frameworks and formulas.
* *Significantly impact your marketplace.*

Values-Based Messaging and Branding:
Develop values-driven messaging and social content using biblically-sound filters.
* *Increase your marketplace influence.*

Online Business Structures and Systems:
Build automation and scale protocols for business optimization.
* *Expand your marketshare.*

QUARTERLY AND MONTHLY PLANS ARE AVAILABLE!

GET ON OUR WAITLIST TO ENROLL!
www.FaithFocusFlow.com/Institute

Successful founders, owners, leaders who are looking to align their business practices with God's purpose, often come to two looming questions:

1. Up until this point in time, has my life been impactful?
2. How significant is my work?

Significance comes with the legacy you build and the lives you ultimately touch.

Our clients seek to infuse Kingdom principles into their industries and marketplaces.

At the FaithFocusFlow® Institute for Leaders, we are committed to helping our clients ALIGN their work with their faith to significantly impact the marketplace and expand their market share.

This is what we do and we'd love to do it for you. Join us!